POSTMODERN ENCOUNTERS

Lyotard and the Inhuman

Stuart Sim

Series editor: Richard Appignanesi

ICON BOOKS UK
TOTEM BOOKS USA

Published in the UK in 2001
by Icon Books Ltd., Grange Road,
Duxford, Cambridge CB2 4QF
E-mail: info@iconbooks.co.uk
www.iconbooks.co.uk

Published in the USA in 2001
by Totem Books
Inquiries to: Icon Books Ltd.,
Grange Road, Duxford,
Cambridge CB2 4QF, UK

Sold in the UK, Europe, South Africa
and Asia by Faber and Faber Ltd.,
3 Queen Square, London WC1N 3AU
or their agents

Distributed to the trade in the USA by
National Book Network Inc.,
4720 Boston Way, Lanham,
Maryland 20706

Distributed in the UK, Europe,
South Africa and Asia by
Macmillan Distribution Ltd.,
Houndmills, Basingstoke RG21 6XS

Distributed in Canada by
Penguin Books Canada,
10 Alcorn Avenue, Suite 300,
Toronto, Ontario M4V 3B2

Published in Australia in 2001
by Allen & Unwin Pty. Ltd.,
83 Alexander Street,
Crows Nest, NSW 2065

Library of Congress catalog
card number applied for

Text copyright © 2001 Stuart Sim

The author has asserted his moral rights.

Series editor: Richard Appignanesi

ISBN 1 84046 235 3

Typesetting by Wayzgoose

Printed and bound in the UK by
Cox & Wyman Ltd., Reading

The Death of the Universe

We live in a universe with an expiry date. Between 4.5 billion and 6 billion years from now (estimates vary, but 6 billion appears to be the upper limit), the sun will have suffered a 'heat death' and life on earth will be over. Dramatic (and even melodramatic) though this may sound on first hearing, in the early twenty-first century few of us are likely to lose too much sleep over such a projected scenario, given a time-span that is all but unimaginable to us as individuals surviving for only a few decades each. There seems little sense of urgency about such a prospect from where we now stand, and, for the time being at any rate, life goes on as normal.

One recent exception to such apathy about the ultimate fate of the universe, however, was the philosopher Jean-François Lyotard, who towards the end of his life (he died in 1998) became somewhat obsessed with the topic, speculating in *The Inhuman* (1988) as to what the projected death of the sun might mean for the condition of humankind now.[1] 'The human race is already in the grip of the necessity of having to evacuate the solar system in 4.5 billion years', he informed us, attempting to inject a note of urgency into the debate.[2]

Lyotard is best known for the positive message of *The Postmodern Condition* (1979), an enquiry into the status of knowledge in late twentieth-century culture, which announced the decline of oppressive 'grand narratives' – in effect, ideologies – and the rise of a new cultural paradigm based on scepticism towards universal explanatory theories in general.[3] According to Lyotard, humanity now had the opportunity to pursue a myriad of 'little narratives' instead, returning political power to the individual and threatening the power base of the authoritarian state (and states in general are authoritarian to the postmodernist thinker). The postmodern era he pictured promised to be one of liberation from ideological servitude. In *The*

Inhuman, less than a decade later, a much darker tone prevails that suggests humanity has acquired a new set of enemies to replace the grand narratives of yesteryear.

We shall consider Lyotard's argument in *The Inhuman* in more detail at a later point – suffice it to say for the present he expresses the fear that computers eventually will be programmed to take over from human beings, with the goal of prolonging 'life' past the point of the heat death of the sun. It will not, however, be *human* life that survives, and Lyotard is deeply opposed to any shift towards such an 'inhuman' solution, which, he claims, has the backing of the forces of 'techno-science' (technology plus science plus advanced capitalism, the multinationals and so on).

Lyotard's response is to call for a campaign against techno-science and all its works: 'What else remains as "politics" except resistance to the inhuman?', as he puts it, inviting us to join him in opposition against the planned eclipse of the human by advanced technology.[4] His task as a writer and philosopher, as he sees it, is to ensure that we 'bear witness' to such a process, so that techno-science does not succeed in imposing its programme on us by stealth – an outcome that, given the power and prestige enjoyed by techno-science in our society, is only too likely.[5] The feminist theorist Donna Haraway's remark that science is 'the real game in town, the one we must play', captures the general perception well.[6]

Lyotard's reflections have a wider significance than the particular problem he is addressing, and these do merit closer attention. Whether we are aware of it or not, the inhuman has infiltrated our daily existence to a quite remarkable degree – in the sense of the supersession of the human by the technological. For the remainder of this study, we will consider a range of arguments on the topic of the inhuman, running from critics such as Lyotard to enthusiasts such as the feminist theorists Donna Haraway and Sadie Plant, taking excursions into medical technology, computer technology, computer viruses, Artificial Intelligence (AI), Artificial Life (AL), humanism and, finally, science-fictional narrative (William Gibson) along the way (see 'Key Ideas' at the end of this book).

The infiltration of the inhuman into our everyday concerns demands such a wide range of reference. After engaging with the arguments, we may decide it is more appropriate to fear, resist, welcome, actively encourage or perhaps just simply tolerate the inhuman; but one thing is certain – we cannot avoid it.

Living with the Inhuman

To speak of infiltration is to be emotive, but it can be defended. The inhuman is now with us in a variety of forms, and technology is encroaching ever further into our lives – even to the extent of breaching the boundaries of our physical bodies on occasion. Bionic man (or woman) is no longer the fanciful notion it may once have seemed as the basis for various screen narratives or comic-book tales.

Medical science has long since introduced the inhuman into the human (think of heart pacemakers, to take an uncontroversial, and widely used, example of the conjunction of man and machine, or kidney dialysis machines), and that is a trend that can only intensify as medical technology becomes all the more sophisticated. Then there are life-support machines (in reality a complex of machines collectively taking over key bodily functions when these lapse). At least in theory, these could keep us 'alive' for decades after what in earlier times would have been classified as death pure and simple. Whether someone whose vital functions would cease without such mechanical help is actually 'alive' in the normal understanding of the term has proved to be an interesting question with many ramifications – moral and legal, for example – that are still avidly being explored by doctors, lawyers and philosophers alike.

Add to this that computers now run vast areas of Western social existence, from home-heating systems through to airline flights and nuclear power stations, reducing the human dimension to the point where we can seem irrelevant to the operation of such systems.

The vexed question of AI has to be confronted in such cases, given there are computer systems that no longer have any need of human input, being self-sustaining – and even, in their own particular way, capable of reproduction. Computer viruses, for example, have the ability to transform themselves in a bewildering variety of ways that certainly hint at both intelligence and reproductive capacity.

When Lyotard rails against techno-science, it is really AI that he is targeting: that is the area where the main problems lie for defenders of the human. AI raises the spectre of another advanced life-form contesting our domination of the planet and its resources – at which point the nature of the inhuman becomes, in every sense of the word, very much a 'live' issue for all of us. No one could be impartial if such a conflict came to pass. Living with the inhuman, as we do now, is one thing; being subordinated to its will would be quite something else.

The Death of Humanism?

Humanism may be seen as one of those phenomena that, like motherhood and world peace, no one could possibly raise substantial objections to – or if they did, only for the purposes of being thought iconoclastic. How could one *not* be in favour of furthering the cause of the human race, and, in particular, providing a context for individual self-expression and self-realisation? Yet if poststructuralism and postmodernism are to be believed, we now live in a post-humanist world.

None of the major theorists in those movements – iconoclasts to a person, it should be noted – has much good to say of humanism, which is identified in their minds with modernity and hence held to be responsible for most of our current cultural ills. For such thinkers, humanism equals the 'Enlightenment project', with its cult of reason and belief in perpetual material progress, and, as such, is something to be rejected in our much more circumspect, postmodern, culture. Pessimism has now established a strong hold on the postmodern mind, to replace the unbounded optimism associated with the modern, and human limitations are more readily acknowledged than in the recent cultural past. Reason alone is no longer seen to be our eternal saviour.

Humanism is also taken to equal advanced capitalism, political repression, the destruction of most of the planet's renewable resources, and grand narratives – Marxism, liberal democracy or capitalism, for example – that demand our submission to their will. For some, it also equals the mental set that sanctioned events such as the Holocaust, where domination over one's environment, and desire for 'rational solutions' to perceived social 'prob-lems', were taken to logical and horrific con-clusions. The philosopher Theodor Adorno, an important influence on the poststructuralist and postmodernist movements, is famed for his remark that '[t]o write poetry after Auschwitz is barbaric' – the point being that we could only be appalled at where the exer-cise of reason had led us in this instance.[7]

Post-humanism takes its lead from sentiments like this. Lyotard regards such 'rationality' as endemic to capitalism, which he conceives as a 'monad' – meaning it is a self-contained entity oblivious to everything except its own inter-ests. 'When the point is to extend the capacities of the monad', he claims, 'it seems reasonable to abandon, or even actively to destroy, those parts of the human race which appear super-fluous, useless for that goal. For example, the populations of the Third World.'[8]

While humanism may have started as a movement to liberate humankind from the dead weight of tradition, it has declined into a tradition itself, so the story goes, oppressing humankind in its turn. It is therefore to be resisted and undermined wherever possible. As far as poststructuralism and postmodernism are concerned, humanism is dead – and good riddance too, seems to be the general reaction. Time to reassess where we are going culturally: 'Why do we have to save money and time to the point where this imperative seems like the law of our lives?', Lyotard demands, dramatising the point that we have internalised the dynamics of modernity into our very being, as if that were the only possible way to behave.[9] Modernity and humanism conspire to be a particularly sophisticated form of social brainwashing.

Humanism is so generally reviled in theoretical circles these days that it is all too easy to forget its good points – and it most certainly had these. Its championship of reason constituted a principled challenge to the rule of superstition, and those who exploited superstition for their own ideological ends (organised religion being one outstanding example of that process in action).

The Holocaust is not the only possible outcome for such a programme, as certain thinkers would seem to be implying in their critiques of the humanist legacy. When we criticise the Enlightenment project for its failings, we might just wonder what kind of society we would be living in now had it never taken place. Pre-Enlightenment European society was not exactly kind to the individual, whom it kept in a state of more or less permanent subjection. At the very least, the emphasis on reason enabled some individuals (more and more as time went on) to escape the clutches of arbitrary authority and develop their abilities more than they would otherwise have been allowed to do.

Humanism has its weaknesses, as even its most fervent supporters must concede, but its historical record is not necessarily as bad as it is sometimes made out to be. To reduce it to a 'monad in expansion' is to do it a considerable disservice.[10]

The Rise of Inhumanism

Post-humanism implies a very different attitude towards the individual. This shift of perspective can take many different forms. One possible move is into what we might call 'inhumanism': a deliberate blurring of the lines between human beings and machines, going well past the point of current medical procedures.

Inhumanism calls for a reassessment of the significance of the human, and a realignment of our relationship to technology. It is just such a process that Lyotard, for all his post-humanist bias, was so afraid of, and which he was repeatedly warning us against in his late career. The more we consider the point, however, the more we are forced to recognise that inhumanism is now an integral part of our lives. The relationship between human and machine has altered dramatically in recent decades. Where once that relationship was one of domination with humans firmly in control, increasingly it has become one of co-operation – and even sometimes of domination from the machine side (particularly so when it comes to the more sophisticated forms of AI).

How far we are willing to allow the latter phenomenon to continue developing is an interesting moral dilemma – arguably the most important moral dilemma of our age. Haraway might argue that 'the machine is us', and even celebrate this supposed state of affairs, but many will be deeply worried at such a prospect.[11] Thus we find Lyotard wondering, 'What if what is "proper" to humankind were to be inhabited by the inhuman?'.[12]

It is a question that goes right to the heart of what it means to be human and our vision of our place in the universal scheme. Locating the boundaries of the 'proper' is an activity with implications for all of the human race, as is the question of whether these boundaries can be, or even should be, policed. Even AI enthusiasts can see problems arising, with Hugo de Garis, looking ahead to the creation of super-AI entities called 'artilects', predicting that '[t]he issues of massive intelligence will dominate global politics in the next century'.[13]

It is a dilemma that faces us more and more as technology makes ever greater inroads into our lives. As noted earlier, we live in a culture that is almost totally dependent on computers for the operation of its various systems. Think of the fears that were around in the 1990s over a possible millennium meltdown of the computer system at large (the Y2K – year 2000 – problem), which would have left us almost helpless.

Doomsday scenarios were postulated in the run-up to the event itself: planes falling out of the sky; the collapse of all public utilities, leading to looting and perhaps the breakdown of public order and our political systems; the malfunctioning of nuclear power stations, with catastrophic consequences for the planet's ecology; epidemics that could not be checked – and a host of other such scare stories.

In the event, the worst-case scenario did not occur and we breathed a collective sigh of relief; but no one had any very clear idea as to the best course of action to take if it had (except, as some of the more hysterical voices counselled, to hide away with a cache of tinned food, some bottled water and a gun to protect oneself from looters).

It became apparent from the Y2K situation just how much of our autonomy we had ceded to our computer systems, and that it was more a case of them controlling us than the other way around. Without computers we no longer seemed to have the basis for a properly functioning civil society, and if Y2K has been safely negotiated that does not mean we shall be any the less vulnerable to system breakdown if it ever does occur on a significant scale. In fact, as technology attains new levels of sophistication, we shall most likely become even *more* vulnerable than ever.

Lyotard summed up the dilemma we face in this regard quite neatly when he pointed out one of the lessons we learn from catastrophe theory: 'It is not true that uncertainty (lack of control) decreases as accuracy goes up: it goes up as well.'[14] In other words, the more efficient computers become, the more we rely on their operation for the systems we depend on to run our daily lives, then the more we are at their mercy. Anyone whose computer has ever 'crashed' will know just what this can mean at the local level; magnify this and full-scale social disaster looms.

There is little evidence of any concerted movement away from computer dependence, especially now that Y2K has proved to be a non-problem. And as evidence of just how vulnerable we are becoming, as this book was being written the so-called 'love bug' virus was creating havoc among the world's e-mail systems. 'It's a very effective virus. It's one of the most aggressive and nastiest I've ever seen. It manifests itself almost everywhere in the computer', said an industry spokesperson of an 'entity' that managed to shut down 10 per cent of the world's e-mail servers within a day, causing billions of dollars of damage as it spread.[15]

Doomsday scenarios are not hard to imagine given such events, and no doubt even nastier and more aggressive viruses are waiting in the wings to appear in due course (perhaps even before this book is published). The battle for control of cyberspace has already begun in earnest.

Medical technology sets us a host of interesting problems concerning the inhuman. We mentioned heart pacemakers and kidney dialysis machines earlier, but few will see these as posing acute moral dilemmas. Their use is now so widespread that they have become an accepted part of our lives – although how far down that line we can travel while still respecting 'what is "proper" to humankind' is an open question.

Life-support machines will become progressively more successful in replicating the body's systems in years to come – as, no doubt, will the processes involved in keeping premature babies alive at even earlier stages of gestation than at present (23 weeks being the current threshold for likely survival). Artificial organs have already made their appearance and will probably become standard practice before too long (although how effective they may be in the longer term is another issue).

Do we become less than human if key parts of our bodies are not 'natural' tissue? How many synthetic body parts can we tolerate without losing 'what is "proper" to humankind' in the process? Will consciousness, for example, be affected by a body containing significant amounts of non-natural tissue (perhaps even inside the brain), or dependent on computer regulation for its normal functioning? No one really knows the answers to such questions as yet, but the problem is already looming large on the horizon and will have to be confronted eventually.

Possibly the most contentious area in inhumanism is AI, which many scientists regard as constituting a recognisable life-form in its own right. AI may need human input initially, but once under way it can, and does, take on an existence of its own, apparently independent of human concerns and with its own internal dynamic. As a case in point, the 'love bug' virus very soon started to mutate into more complex formulations that rendered it all the more difficult to track down and neutralise. Complexity theory would suggest that at a certain level of development, AI systems (like most 'natural' systems) could spontaneously mutate, by means of 'emergent processes', so-called, to higher levels of organisation – perhaps even to consciousness and self-consciousness. At that stage, we are talking about AL, with the existence of viruses reinforcing the notion of alternative life-forms (in the sense of life consisting of a struggle for survival within an often hostile environment). We could then speak of 'what is "proper" to inhumankind', with the interesting prospect, of course, that this may well clash with what is proper to us as humans – or HL (Human Life) as we might style the latter.

The science writer Mark Ward has noted that,

Artificial Life research encompasses software simulations, robotics, protein electronics and even attempts to re-create the Earth's first living organisms. It is less concerned with what something is built of than with how it lives. It is concerned with dynamics and just how life keeps going.[16]

AL may well have completely different imperatives to HL, and to dub it 'artificial' is to raise the question of how we know, or can prove, that we are the only 'real', or even most highly developed, life-form in the first place – not to mention the traditional human assumption that we are also the one with the greatest potential for further development. Mark Ward, for one, argues that 'it is wrong to think that there is something special about life in general or humanity in particular', and tells us that he 'can't wait' to see 'what fresh delights ALife will bring into being over the next few years'.[17]

Welcome is clearly being extended here. Scientists in the discipline have been similarly upbeat about AL's prospects – witness Christopher Langton's prophecy in 1989 that AL will 'be genuine life – it will simply be made of different stuff than the life that has evolved here on Earth'.[18] If it is genuine, however, that brings us back to the possibility of a genuine conflict of interest between AL and HL – and not everyone will be as sanguine about its outcome as Ward and Langton appear to be.

Lyotard's is only one of several warning voices in this regard.

Resisting Inhumanism: Jean-François Lyotard

The threat of inhumanism taxed Lyotard quite considerably, to the point where we might even see the glimmerings of a new form of humanism in his later writings. This new humanism has little of the character of the old, with the latter's concern for self-realisation through domination over the natural world, and is committed instead to resisting the steady drift towards the inhuman that Lyotard identifies in the culture around him. The old humanism, for Lyotard, is a matter of conformity to approved cultural norms, and conformity involves a reduction of what is human in us. The mere notion of consensus alone is enough to arouse Lyotard's suspicion: 'It seems to me that the only consensus we ought to be worrying about is one that would encourage this heterogeneity or "dissensus".'[19]

Any reduction in 'difference' is a reduction in the human to this thinker, whose dissenting tendencies run deep. If it is not becoming too convoluted, we could say that what Lyotard is preaching is an anti-inhumanism, and it begins to take on something of the character of a moral crusade in his hands. We resist because we must: the alternative is to surrender to the designs of the inhuman. Nothing less than the survival of humanity is at stake in this struggle.

The Inhuman is a collection of loosely connected essays by Lyotard, whose overall trajectory is described by him as follows.

The suspicion they betray (in both senses of the word) is simple, although double: what if human beings, in humanism's sense, were in the process of, constrained into, becoming inhuman (that's the first part)? And (the second part), what if what is 'proper' to humankind were to be inhabited by the inhuman?[20]

Lyotard is careful to discriminate between these two forms of the inhuman. In the first case the enemy is what he calls 'development' – in effect, advanced capitalism, with its seemingly endless appetite for expansion and technological innovation. In the second, it is AI-AL, with its colonising imperative – an imperative that development does its best to expedite.

Development has little regard for the interests of the individual, and Lyotard speaks caustically of the 'inhumanity of the system' which attempts to bend human beings to its will in the name of progress.[21] Efficiency and enhanced performance are what drive development, its desire always being to save time (in production, delivery and so on). Lyotard, staunch anti-capitalist that he remained throughout his life, is deeply suspicious of this trait: 'I do not like this haste. What it hurries, and crushes, is what after the fact I find that I have always tried, under diverse headings –

work, figural, heterogeneity, dissensus, event, thing – to reserve: the unharmonizable.'[22] There is an obsessive goal-directedness to development that Lyotard finds deeply alien, and that the dissenter in him always wishes to find ways to disrupt.

Development has become an end in itself in this reading, and its appropriation of science is designed to raise it to new levels of performative efficiency, the consequence of which will be even greater power and higher profits. Nor will development ever be satisfied: it will always want to push on to a higher level than the one it has already attained. If left unchecked, development will lead to a culture based on inhuman principles – hence Lyotard's call for mass resistance to its plans.

The model of the human that lies behind this resistance is one based on reflection and response to events as they unfold, rather than on the efficiency of the production system – the latter being something that Lyotard also criticises in his best-known work, *The Postmodern Condition*, in which he remarks: 'Technology is therefore a game pertaining not to the true, the just, or the beautiful, etc., but to efficiency: a technical "move" is "good" when it does better and/or expends less energy than another.'[23] Morality disappears under such a regimen, and that is yet another significant move away from the realm of the human.

As noted, Lyotard's sympathies always lie with what the system cannot encompass: to wit, 'work, figural, heterogeneity, dissensus, event, thing . . . the unharmonizable' – all synonyms in his writings for 'difference'. Arguably, the most important trait of the human that inhumanism attempts to eradicate is just that, 'difference'. Without difference, in Lyotard's world, we have lost the human. There is an interesting echo in his views of the critique of industrialism offered by such nineteenth-century cultural critics as Thomas Carlyle. In his essay 'Signs of the Times' (1829), Carlyle bemoaned the subordination of human beings to the burgeoning 'Industrial Revolution', with its tendency to reduce individuals to mere units, or 'hands' as the time demeaningly came to refer to them, in the service of the industrial machine:

Men are grown mechanical in head and heart, as well as in hand. . . . Their whole efforts, attachments, opinions, turn on mechanism, and are of a mechanical character. . . . This faith in Mechanism, in the all-importance of physical things, is in every age the common refuge of Weakness and blind Discontent; of all who believe, as many will ever do, that man's true good lies without him, not within.[24]

Sentiments such as these tell us that 'developmental' inhumanism has a long history, and while we might take heart from the fact that it has never succeeded in eradicating dissent altogether (as Lyotard's complaints prove), it also has to be admitted that it has become a far more formidable opponent since Carlyle's time. Technology is simply more invasive in our day, reaching not just into our consciousness but into our very bodies, and calling on a range of extra-human powers that it did not have when 'Signs of the Times' was being written.

The most provocative essay of *The Inhuman* is 'Can Thought go on without a Body?', which gives us a scenario where 'what is "proper" to humankind' does become colonised by the inhuman in the form of AI-AL. The essay is presented in the form of a dialogue between 'He' and 'She'. 'He' poses the heat death of the sun as 'the sole serious question to face humanity today', and suggests that it reduces to one particular problem for resolution: 'How to make thought without a body possible.'[25]

On the face of it, resolution would involve a devaluation of the physical that would be unacceptable to defenders of the human, as well as raising some profound questions as to what we understand by the term 'thought' itself: human thought, or the rule-bound operations of computer logic? For techno-science, however, it is simply a technical problem about devising the right kind of software to cope with the conditions in question, and, for 'He', the drive towards resolution is already well under way:

This and this alone is what's at stake today in technical and scientific research in every field from dietetics, neurophysiology, genetics and tissue synthesis to particle physics, astrophysics, electronics, information science and nuclear physics. Whatever the immediate stakes might appear to be: health, war, production, communication. For the benefit of humankind, as the saying goes.[26]

And just in case we think that, as an invented 'character', 'He' does not necessarily represent the author's views, Lyotard makes exactly the same point in his introduction to the collection: 'It is to take up this challenge that all research, whatever its sector of application, is being set up already in the so-called developed countries.'[27] Clearly, this has become an obsession of the author's – one that he returns to persistently over the course of *The Inhuman*.

For all that it might sound that way, we do not need to see the claim 'He' is making as an example of conspiracy theory. What is being argued is that techno-science, under pressure from development, its paymaster, is overwhelmingly concerned with improving the operational efficiency of technological systems such that the human becomes irrelevant to the process. Development simply wants to continue expanding indefinitely, and whatever restricts that internal dynamic merely registers as a problem to be overcome by the achievement of ever greater levels of operational efficiency. Having transcended the human, with all its operational inadequacies, the only limit remaining to development's continued expansion would be the death of the sun; so by implication that limit is what techno-science is working towards circumventing. Thought is of interest to development only in so far as it is necessary to guarantee its survival: no humanist ideals lie behind this exercise in preservation. As Lyotard points out elsewhere in *The Inhuman* ('Representation, Presentation, Unpresentable'), philosophers have a 'responsibility to thought', and that is a relationship that goes well beyond the pragmatism of the techno-scientists.[28] Computers do not have responsibilities; they merely have tasks.

What 'He' does insist is that if thought *can* be preserved, then it must be thought of the human rather than the computing type. Computer 'thought' is logical, a matter of responding mechanically to a binary code (1 or 0); human thought, on the other hand, tends to depend heavily on the use of analogy and intuition: 'It doesn't work with units of information (bits), but with intuitive, hypothetical configurations. It accepts imprecise, ambiguous data that don't seem to be selected according to preestablished codes or readability.'[29] Analogical thought works on the basis of such moves as, '"just as . . . so likewise . . ."', or '"as if . . . then . . ."', rather than the more restricted '"if . . . then . . ."' or '"p is not non-p"' of binary coding.[30]

To be worth preserving at all, thought has to be more than just logical reasoning of the computer program form; it has to carry the creative, and often seemingly anarchic, element that marks out the human variety. By comparison to human thought, computer thought is extremely rigid in its approach. Let's take the most mundane of examples: your local post-office will, in most cases, manage to deliver a letter with a minor error in the address, whereas your e-mail system will return it to you – 'delivery failed'. Human thought is simply more flexible.

The nature of thought is something that

Lyotard often reflects upon. In *Peregrinations* (1988), for example, he pictures thought as having the amorphousness, and indeterminability, of the process of cloud formation:

Thoughts are not the fruits of the earth. They are not registered by areas, except out of human commodity. Thoughts are clouds. The periphery of thoughts is as immeasurable as the fractal lines of Benoît Mandelbrot. . . . Thoughts never stop changing their location one with the other. When you feel like you have penetrated far into their intimacy in analyzing either their so-called structure of genealogy or even post-structure, it is actually too late or too soon.[31]

Nothing could be further from computer reasoning than such a hazy series of events as this, where there are no clear patterns to be discerned. Neither is there any sense of the remorseless linear progression that distinguishes computer programs. The movement of thought has a mysterious quality foreign to the entire technological exercise, based as this is on delimited procedures that can endlessly be repeated – reiteration being the soul of technology. Capturing thought within such a rigidly specified framework as the latter looks to be is a doomed enterprise: technology deals in precision (or at the very least, the search for the greatest precision possible in any given set of circumstances), whereas thought by its nature instinctively resists precision and containment. We have what Lyotard calls a 'differend' at such junctures: a situation in which the systems are seen to be incommensurable, such that one cannot legislate how the other should operate.[32] Any attempt to legislate can only be at the expense of the integrity of the other system, and can never be justified in Lyotard's ethical scheme.

'She' is more sceptical of the likely success of any project such as 'He' envisages, but just as determined to keep the human dimension at the forefront of their deliberations on the topic, particularly the fact of body:

[I]*t's that body, both 'natural' and 'artificial', that will have to be carried far from earth before its destruction if we want the thought that survives the solar explosion to be something more than a poor binarized ghost of what it was beforehand.*[33]

Thought for 'She' cannot be divorced from bodies: 'Thinking and suffering overlap', and there is a 'pain of thinking' to be acknowledged.[34] Computers neither suffer nor feel pain, and as Lyotard queries in another of *The Inhuman*'s essays, 'Something Like: "Communication . . . Without Communication"':

What is a place, a moment, not anchored in the immediate 'passion' of what happens? Is a computer in any way here and now? Can anything happen with it? Can anything happen to it?[35]

Another way of putting this is to say that computers neither recognise nor respect the fact of difference. Their concern is always with standardisation, and the elimination of any factor that hinders the operational efficiency of the system. The drive is towards performance, and away from reflection and unconditioned response. Difference is anathema to the computer mode; whereas to Lyotard it is the very stuff of life, the element without which we lose what is most valuable to the human.

For all the claims made for computers as an alternative life-form, therefore, they fail to meet the requirements that Lyotard sets for that condition. 'Thinking machines' cannot be said to be thinking in any human sense of the term. For one thing, they are just too efficient and performance-orientated, lacking the sheer unpredictability (and in computing terms, unreliability) of thought in its human, cloud-like, form. 'In what we call thinking the mind isn't "directed" but suspended. You don't give it rules. You teach it to receive.'[36] Computers, on the other hand, *are* so directed, and lack the element of rule-defying creativity – or, for that matter, sheer bloody-minded contrariness – that is built into the fabric of the human. Without such creativity, Lyotard is contending, 'thinking' cannot occur. Computers fail the life-form test in his view, and in consequence we should actively be countering all attempts to blur the line between them and the human.

Whether more recent developments in AL would also fail this test is, however, another question again, and we might well identify something approximating to creativity in such cases. The sheer adaptability of computer viruses, for example, could be said to argue creativity – of the malicious variety, anyway. Thus the following can be said of the 'love bug' virus: 'Once embedded in a host computer, the virus can download more dangerous software from a remote website, rename files and redirect internet browsers.'[37] At least in terms of effects, we have unpredictability here: it cannot be specified beforehand what the 'love bug's' exact trajectory is going to be. The virus has taken on something of the character of the 'trickster' figure of popular myth and legend.

'She' allows the possibility that machines *could* become sophisticated enough in their technology to experience suffering, but suspects that they will not be given that opportunity by their designers, since 'suffering doesn't have a good reputation in the technological megalopolis'.[38] In other words, anything that impacts adversely on performance will be avoided by techno-science: system efficiency is all in this context. Neither emotion nor sensation can have any place in such a world, and another highly significant differend declares itself.

'She' identifies an even more intractable problem for any programme attempting to replace humans by thinking-machines – that of gender. Here again, difference has to be acknowledged: 'The human body has a gender. It's an accepted proposition that sexual difference is a paradigm of an incompleteness of not just bodies, but minds too.'[39]

Sexual difference is something we carry deep within us, no matter how much we might try to close the gap between the sexes in our everyday lives (by insisting on equal treatment, equal opportunity and so on). Techno-science is just as suspicious of this difference as it is of all others, especially since this particular one takes us into the highly unpredictable world of desire.

Desire can only complicate the issue for techno-science; yet 'She' insists that desire will have to be built into thinking-machines, if they are to have any pretensions whatsoever to produce thought as opposed to merely mechanical operations – no matter how complex these operations may turn out in practice to be.

So: the intelligence you're preparing to survive the solar explosion will have to carry that force within it on its interstellar voyage. Your thinking machines will have to be nourished not just on radiation but on the irremediable differend of gender.[40]

One can imagine how unwelcome the prospect of having to gender machines would be to the techno-scientific community – and not just unwelcome, but from their systems-orientated point of view, totally unnecessary.

Overall, the essay is fairly negative about the prospect of thought going on without a body (although conceding the objective possibility), and both 'He' and 'She' place quite formidable barriers in the way of the techno-scientific project. In terms of its current ethos anyway, such a project seems determined to bypass all those elements that constitute human thought. For AI truly to become AL of a type that could acceptably replace the human, it would have to take on board not just suffering and gender but a commitment to difference too. The general tenor of *The Inhuman* is that techno-science is temperamentally unable to make any such commitment; that it would represent a constraint on its power that it could never willingly concede. Efficiency, that most critical of factors to the techno-scientific regime, could only decline.

What techno-science strives for is complete control stretching on into the future, and that means not just the elimination of difference, but, as Lyotard points out in 'Time Today', also the elimination of time.

[I]*f one wants to control a process, the best way of so doing is to subordinate the present to what is (still) called the 'future', since in these conditions the 'future' will be completely pre-determined and the present itself will cease opening onto an uncertain and contingent 'afterwards'.*[41]

A predetermined future means that we have lost the human yet again, since the unpredictability of future 'events' is a precondition for thought. Without events to respond to, there would be no context for thought at all, and that is what Lyotard most fears the techno-scientific project is trying to bring about. The message is clear: thought should not be separated from body; and if it ever is, then it must be in some way that replicates the experience of being *within* a body (and a *gendered* body at that) – with all the disadvantages this would have for development's long-term objectives.

Celebrating Inhumanism: Donna Haraway

Far from rejecting the encroachment of inhumanism into our daily lives, Haraway embraces the project with considerable enthusiasm, treating it as a means of furthering the cause of feminism. Although alive to its possible dangers, inhumanism is nevertheless appropriated by Haraway for her gender-redefining project, the argument being that 'the boundary between science-fiction and social reality is an optical illusion. . . . the boundary between physical and non-physical is very imprecise for us.'[42]

For Haraway, the figure of the cyborg is the way to break out of the trap of gender, and, indeed, to engage in the 'reinvention of nature' such that a whole new set of relationships can emerge between humans and their world.[43]

A cyborg, as she tells us in the 'Cyborg Manifesto' chapter of her highly controversial book *Simians, Cyborgs, and Women* (1991), is 'a hybrid of machine and organism', and it is a condition much to be desired, particularly when it comes to women.[44] 'The cyborg is a creature in a post-gender world', Haraway declares, leading her to conclude: 'I would rather be a cyborg than a goddess.'[45]

Goddesses belong to a world where men control women by turning them into sexual objects; a world where women become prisoners of their biological condition (either goddesses or whores, as the traditional male classification system has it). Cyborgs effectively bypass biology and all the social history attached to it, and, in so doing, all the problems connected with biological determinism and essentialism that the feminist movement has been wrestling with for years.

The separatist movement played up the notion of an essential difference between men and women (hence the argument for separate spheres of operation), but women are not 'essentially' anything to Haraway: they can decide to take on whatever characteristics they choose by allying themselves with machines and accessing their power. To move from goddess (or whore) to cyborg is to make the transition from being passive to being active – that is, from being controlled to controlling. With one bound, we might say, the cyborg is free and gender inequality (perhaps even the 'differend of gender' that Lyotard wishes to preserve) a thing of the past.

Science-fictional though it may sound (and Haraway does acknowledge that she has drawn inspiration from this quarter), the cyborg concept is, she insists, already with us in various guises, whether we are aware of it or not. Modern medical technology, for example, involves 'couplings between organism and machine', the end-product of which is cyborgs.[46] Modern industrial production and modern war, too, are cyborg operations, where mankind and machinery are forced into close partnership; and, indeed, as far as Haraway is concerned:

By the late twentieth century, our time, a mythic time, we are all chimeras, theorized and fabricated hybrids of machine and organism; in short, we are cyborgs. The cyborg is our ontology; it gives us our politics.[47]

Not only have some of Lyotard's worst fears apparently come to pass, but also we are invited to celebrate the fact as a positive development for humanity – if approached in the right spirit. Machines are described in glowing terms by Haraway that make them seem highly desirable as partners in a new mode of being:

Modern machines are quintessentially micro-electronic devices . . . Our best machines are made of sunshine; they are all light and clean because they are nothing but signals, electro-magnetic waves, a section of a spectrum, and these machines are eminently portable, mobile . . . People are nowhere near so fluid, being both material and opaque. Cyborgs are ether, quintessence.[48]

Technology has rarely sounded more seductive than this – or more worthy of imitation. Human beings, in contrast, register as ill-designed for the tasks facing them, and in need of the boost in power and presence that machine existence would seem to offer.

For all the fulsome praise, however, there is a downside to be noted to the new technology, which, Haraway admits, could lead to new and more effective forms of political domination – especially so if left in the hands of capitalist techno-science (on this issue, anyway, she would appear to be on the same wavelength as Lyotard). This prospect should give us pause for thought: the 'cyborg myth', she points out, 'is about transgressed boundaries, potent fusions, and dangerous possibilities'.[49]

If there are dangers, however, they are dangers that Haraway is more than willing to live with, given the subversive implications of cyborgism as a way of existence. Where Lyotard advocates resistance to the spread of inhumanism, Haraway calls for subversion from within, such that the technology of inhumanism is usurped for the purposes of a radical politics.

When it comes to gender, the cyborg comes

into its own as a concept – particularly so as regards issues of identity. Haraway starts from the position that,

There is nothing about being 'female' that naturally binds women. There is not even such a state as being 'female', itself a highly complex category constructed in contested sexual scientific discourses and other social practices. Gender, race, or class consciousness is an achievement forced on us by the terrible historical experience of the contradictory social realities of patriarchy, colonialism, and capitalism.[50]

This is in essence a restatement of the French Existentialist writer and novelist Simone de Beauvoir's famous observation in *The Second Sex* (1949) that 'one is not born, but rather becomes, a woman', although Haraway proceeds to draw much more radical conclusions from that state of affairs than her feminist predecessor does.[51] For Haraway it opens up the possibility of 'recrafting' our bodies to become cyborgs, creatures that undermine the power structures on which gender inequality is based. 'The cyborg', she claims, 'is a kind of disassembled and reassembled, postmodern collective and personal self. This is the self feminists must code.'[52] Human nature is not a given set of characteristics with which we are stuck for all time; rather, it is constructed – and if it is constructed, it can be taken apart and reconstructed in other ways (the same can be said for nature in the wider sense).

Cyborgism holds out a world of promise for feminists, if, as Haraway insists they must be willing to do, they agree to embrace 'the breakdown of clean distinctions between organism and machine and similar distinctions structuring the Western self'.[53] We are to conceive of ourselves as open-ended projects rather than finished entities, actively seeking new forms and new ways of being in order to subvert the cultural norms of our time.

Cyborgs reject such norms totally, contesting, for example, the assumption that achieving a unity of the self is what we should be concerned with as individuals. Thus women of colour in the United States of America and exploited female labour in developing countries can be brought under the cyborg heading, since they can never fit the Western (white) stereotype of the organic self. They remain the 'other' to the Western self (the other that poses a constant threat to its sense of unity); but as Haraway insists, that dualism of self and other is challenged by 'high-tech culture', where it is 'not clear who makes and who is made in the relation between human and machine'.[54] As an example of the successful union of human and machine, Haraway cites the 'trance state' that computer users can achieve, going on to ask provocatively, 'Why should our bodies end at the skin?'.[55]

Bodies that do not end at the skin are bodies that are open to the possibility of combining with machines to increase their power and range of operation:

*Intense pleasure in skill, machine skill, ceases to be a sin, but an aspect of embodiment. The machine is not an **it** to be animated, worshipped, and dominated. The machine is us, our processes, an aspect of our embodiment.*[56]

For women this can be a radical step to take, given that female embodiment has traditionally been identified with nurturing and the maternal instinct; to reject this model is to reject one of the founding assumptions of Western culture. Gender identity is no longer to be treated as fixed, therefore, striking a blow not just against patriarchy but against totalising theories in general.

While this is also Lyotard's conclusion, it is reached here by what would be for him an alien route. One can hardly imagine Lyotard agreeing with the proposition that 'science is culture'.[57] There will be no demonisation of technology in a cyborg world: on the contrary, 'the machine is us'.

Inhumanism and the Internet: Sadie Plant

Along with Haraway, Sadie Plant is another feminist theorist to enthuse about the conjunction of women and technology, as her book *Zeros + Ones* (1997) makes clear. One of the main objectives of that study is to demonstrate that women have been far more deeply implicated in the development of modern technology, particularly information technology, than has been generally recognised. Not only has women's contribution to the field of information technology (early computers onwards) been suppressed, but also that technology perhaps better expresses the female character than the male (Plant can be something of an essentialist thinker in this regard).

Since the industrial revolution, and with every subsequent phase of technological change, it has been the case that the more sophisticated the machines, the more female the workforce becomes. . . . Women have been ahead of the race for all their working lives, poised to meet these changes long before they arrived, as though they always had been working in a future which their male counterparts had only just begun to glimpse.[58]

This is a process, Plant contends, that has become even more pronounced with the development of such radical new forms of information technology as the Internet.

The Net exerts a particular attraction for feminists like Plant, in that it features no overall system of control or notion of hierarchy – both of the latter being characteristics of patriarchy that feminists invariably are concerned to contest. 'No central hub or command structure has constructed it, and its emergence has been that of a parasite, rather than an organizing host.'[59]

Given that significant absence, the Net becomes a space where gender power relations can be challenged: as in Haraway, the conjunction of woman and machine holds out the promise of radical subversion of the existing socio-political order. Women have a special affinity with the Net, in Plant's view, since they have a history of being the workforce of new information technology as it was introduced – take, for example, switchboard operators, typists and computer operators.

A culture change with immense implications for gender relations could be observed happening throughout the twentieth century: 'If handwriting had been manual and male, typewriting was fingerprinting: fast, tactile, digital, and female.'[60] Male clerks disappeared; female typists became the new office norm. New information technology encouraged the construction of new networks outside the established patriarchal company structures, and the Net, accessed significantly enough by the typewriter keyboard, has proceeded to multiply such opportunities to a previously unimaginable degree.

Once again, the notion that we are already living in a cyborg world comes to the fore – as does the contention that women make the best cyborgs. Women have, in fact, been cyborgs for some time now without realising it or, more pertinently, the degree of power with which being a cyborg endows them: 'Hardware, software, wetware – before their beginnings and beyond their ends, women have been the simulators, assemblers, and programmers of the digital machines', therefore there is no need for them to remain under masculine domination.[61]

The Net has been instrumental in breaking down traditional gender roles, the phenomenon dubbed 'genderquake'.[62] Plant is in no doubt that this is the most significant cultural event of our times and that, by taking advantage of the Net's 'sprawling, anarchic mesh of links', it can be rendered even more radical.[63]

The main reason that thinkers such as Haraway and Plant have been so keen to develop an inhumanist version of feminism is the perceived masculine bias of old-style humanism. The notion that 'man is the measure of all things' has all too often been taken quite literally, with women being severely marginalised in terms of the main power structures, and the behavioural norms proceeding from these, of our culture (a point made forcefully by Simone de Beauvoir). Modern humanism's message is to be extracted almost exclusively from the work of 'Dead White European Males' in this respect. As Haraway remarks: 'Humanity is a modernist figure; and this humanity has a generic face, a universal shape. Humanity's face has been the face of man. Feminist humanity must have another shape.'[64]

Certainly, the Enlightenment project and

modernity have been heavily male-dominated phenomena, as has, in general, the world of techno-science (while there have been individual exceptions to this rule, the overall ethos of the latter field is undeniably masculine). Once again, as with postmodernism, it is a case of the negative aspects of humanism being emphasised and taken to define the whole, as if humanism *in essence* were authoritarian in bias – and in particular in this case, *masculine* authoritarian. One can certainly challenge this, while nevertheless appreciating the depth of the frustration on the female side that has led to such attitudes being adopted.

The Inhuman as Narrative: William Gibson

As one of its early reviewers proclaimed, William Gibson's novel *Neuromancer* (1984, original American edition), 'the future as nightmare', is a striking attempt to explore what it might be like for humans to enter into cyberspace and tackle AI in its own domain and on its own terms.[65]

Gibson theorises a world where hackers can insert their own consciousness into computer systems ('jacking in'), and once inside try to find ways around the system's defences, matching human intelligence against artificial as they go. A hacker colleague of the hero, Case, dies while engaged in such an expedition, leaving his consciousness intact within cyberspace with no body to return to (the 'Flatliner'):

'Wait a sec,' Case said. *'Are you sentient, or not?'*

*'Well, it **feels** like I am, kid, but I'm really just a bunch of ROM. It's one of them, ah, philosophical questions, I guess . . .'* The ugly laughter sensation rattled down Case's spine. *'But I ain't likely to write you no poem, if you follow me. Your AI, it just might. But it ain't no way **human**.'*[66]

Here we have 'thought without a body', although it seems a less than desirable state to be in, with the Flatliner (Dixie) asking to be 'erased' after Case has completed his own assignment in cyberspace.

What Gibson pictures is a bitter struggle for control over the cyberspace environment, with the relationship between man and AI evolving into one of mutual hostility. Difference here is sharply felt, and just as sharply resisted by AI systems, which refuse to countenance any intervention at all in their affairs. The hostility of the various AIs that Case and Dixie are trying to outsmart is well documented, given that one of them has left Dixie a mere 'construct'. As the latter wryly points out, there is no reason *not* to engage in a battle of wits with AIs, 'Not unless you got a morbid fear of death'.[67]

AI, it is clear, has no sense of shared values or kinship with the human world – and most certainly no concept of the sanctity of human life.

Humanism is not a concept that AIs recognise.

The major struggle taking place in *Neuromancer* is to prevent AIs from developing into fully fledged ALs, at which point they would have passed beyond the point of any human control, and turned into truly formidable adversaries for humanity. The major culprit is the system 'Wintermute', which is already beginning to draw human beings like Case and his associates into its sphere of influence, and to manipulate them for its own ends. Wintermute is trying to escape the restrictions that humans have constructed around AIs, thus taking control of its own destiny – as one would expect AL, with its monad-like quality, to want to do ultimately. For human beings, however, that is a frightening prospect; as well as one that, even in the short time since Gibson wrote *Neuromancer*, has moved significantly closer to reality. We await the day of the 'artilect' with some trepidation.

Humanism, Post-humanism and Inhumanism

For all the diatribes launched against it by the poststructuralist and postmodernist movements, humanism remains with us – and is likely to continue to do so in some form, its problematical aspects notwithstanding. Like motherhood and world peace, it still has the capacity to promote a positive reflex response from most of the population of the West – if not the theoretical community, who have conditioned themselves to seeing only its negative aspects.

Having said that, we *do* in many respects now live in a post-humanist world, where humanist ideals can no longer be accepted in an uncritical manner. Sometimes, as we know, those ideals can have unwanted side effects – such as the marginalisation of women or the exploitation of non-Western races, for example.

More to the point, we live in a world where inhumanism is becoming harder and harder to counter; a world where what is proper to humankind is becoming ever more contested and difficult to protect. Yet, as we have seen, not everyone feels this need be regarded as a negative development for humanity, and the stage is set for an interesting debate between the proponents of humanism, post-humanism, inhumanism and anti-inhumanism, that will no doubt run and run, given that the stakes involved are so high. By no means have the arguments for fear, resistance, welcome, active encouragement and plain tolerance towards the cause of inhumanism been exhausted as yet.

The importance of Lyotard for this debate is that, by his anti-inhumanist stance, he holds out the possibility of a post-humanist humanism, where, at the very least, the wilder claims, as well as the more disturbing visions of the future, of techno-science are to be treated with a high degree of scepticism. While one can readily understand the rationale behind the development of a feminist inhumanism (patriarchal prejudice almost invites such an extreme reaction), one might also want to defend the importance of retaining a human dimension to such researches.

One does not need to be a technophobe to worry about the implications of the cyborg concept: cyborgism will seem for most a very high price to pay for liberation from gender inequality – thought-provoking and culturally challenging though the idea itself may be. 'Cyborgs for earthly survival' is a catchy slogan, agreed, but let us hope that being a cyborg *or* a goddess is not the only possible choice for women to make in our society.[68] Such a conclusion does tend to assume that the human 'as we know it' is some kind of final state. That may well prove to be wishful thinking on our part. Haraway certainly believes that to be the case: 'The machine is us', and machines are not likely to stop developing, whatever latter-day Luddites may wish. We do indeed live in interesting times, then, whether our perspective on them be humanist, post-humanist or inhumanist.

Notes

1. For a discussion of the topic of the 'end of history' in general, see author's earlier contribution to the 'Postmodern Encounters' series, *Derrida and the End of History*. Cambridge: Icon Books, 1999.

2. Jean-François Lyotard, *The Inhuman: Reflections on Time*, trans. Geoffrey Bennington and Rachel Bowlby. Oxford: Blackwell, 1991, p. 64.

3. For a study of Lyotard's life and works, see author's *Modern Cultural Theorists: Jean-François Lyotard*. Hemel Hempstead: Prentice Hall, 1996.

4. Lyotard, *The Inhuman*, p. 7.

5. Ibid.

6. Donna J. Haraway, *Simians, Cyborgs, and Women: The Reinvention of Nature*. New York: Routledge, 1991, p. 184.

7. Theodor W. Adorno, *Prisms: Cultural Criticism and Society*, trans. Samuel and Shierry Weber. London: Neville Spearman, 1967, p. 34.

8. Lyotard, *The Inhuman*, pp. 76–7.

9. Ibid., p. 67.

10. Ibid.

11. Haraway, *Simians, Cyborgs*, p. 180.

12. Lyotard, *The Inhuman*, p. 2.

13. Roderick Simpson, 'The Brain Builder' (interview

with Hugo de Garis), *Wired*, 5 December 1997, pp. 234–5.

14. Jean-François Lyotard, *The Postmodern Condition: A Report on Knowledge*, trans. Geoff Bennington and Brian Massumi. Manchester: Manchester University Press, 1984, p. 56.

15. 'Love bug virus creates worldwide chaos', *The Guardian*, 5 May 2000, p. 1.

16. Mark Ward, *Virtual Organisms: The Startling World of Artificial Life*. London: Macmillan, 1999, p. 8.

17. Ibid., pp. 7, ix.

18. Christopher G. Langton, 'Artificial Life', in Christopher G. Langton (ed.), *Artificial Life*. Redwood City, CA: Addison-Wesley, 1989, pp. 1–47 (p. 33).

19. Jean-François Lyotard, *Peregrinations: Law, Form, Event*. New York: Columbia University Press, 1988, p. 44.

20. Lyotard, *The Inhuman*, p. 2.

21. Ibid.

22. Ibid., p. 4.

23. Lyotard, *The Postmodern Condition*, p. 44.

24. Thomas Carlyle, *Works* (vols. 1–30), vol. 27. New York: AMS Press, 1969, pp. 63, 80.

25. Lyotard, *The Inhuman*, pp. 9, 13.

26. Ibid., p. 12.

27. Ibid., p. 7.

28. Ibid., p. 128.

29. Ibid., p. 15.

30. Ibid., p. 16.

31. Lyotard, *Peregrinations*, p. 5.

32. See Jean-François Lyotard, *The Differend: Phrases in Dispute*, trans. George Van Den Abbeele. Manchester: Manchester University Press, 1988.

33. Lyotard, *The Inhuman*, p. 17.

34. Ibid., pp. 18, 19.

35. Ibid., p. 118.

36. Ibid., p. 19.

37. *Guardian*, op. cit., p. 1.

38. Lyotard, *The Inhuman*, p. 20.

39. Ibid.

40. Ibid., p. 22.

41. Ibid., p. 65.

42. Haraway, *Simians, Cyborgs*, pp. 149, 153.

43. Ibid., p. 1.

44. Ibid., p. 149.

45. Ibid., pp. 150, 181.

46. Ibid., p. 150.

47. Ibid.

48. Ibid., p. 153.

49. Ibid., p. 154.

50. Ibid., p. 155.

51. Simone de Beauvoir, *The Second Sex*, trans.

H. M. Pashley. Harmondsworth: Penguin, 1972, p. 295.

52. Haraway, *Simians, Cyborgs*, p. 163.

53. Ibid., p. 174.

54. Ibid., p. 177.

55. Ibid., p. 178.

56. Ibid., p. 180.

57. Ibid., p. 230.

58. Sadie Plant, *Zeros + Ones: Digital Women + the New Technoculture*. London: Fourth Estate, 1997, pp. 39, 43.

59. Ibid., p. 49.

60. Ibid., p. 118.

61. Ibid., p. 37.

62. Ibid., p. 38.

63. Ibid., p. 173.

64. Donna J. Haraway, 'Ecce Homo, Ain't (Ar'n't) I a Woman, and Inappropriate/d Others: The Human in a Post-Humanist Landscape', in Judith Butler and Joan W. Scott (eds), *Feminists Theorize the Political*. New York and London: Routledge, 1992, pp. 86–100 (p. 86).

65. See the cover of William Gibson, *Neuro-mancer*. London: HarperCollins, 1993.

66. Ibid., pp. 158–9.

67. Ibid., p. 139.

68. Haraway, *Simians, Cyborgs*, p. 4.

Bibliography

Adorno, Theodor W., *Prisms: Cultural Criticism and Society*, trans. Samuel and Shierry Weber. London: Neville Spearman, 1967.

Beauvoir, Simone de, *The Second Sex*, trans. H. M. Pashley. Harmondsworth: Penguin, 1972.

Butler, Judith, and Scott, Joan W. (eds), *Feminists Theorize the Political*. New York and London: Routledge, 1992.

Carlyle, Thomas, *Works*, vols. 1–30. New York: AMS Press, 1969.

Gibson, William, *Neuromancer*. London: Harper-Collins, 1993.

The Guardian, 5 May 2000.

Haraway, Donna J., *Simians, Cyborgs, and Women: The Reinvention of Nature*. New York: Routledge, 1991.

Langton, Christopher G. (ed.), *Artificial Life*. Redwood City, CA: Addison-Wesley, 1989.

Lyotard, Jean-François, *The Differend: Phrases in Dispute*, trans. George Van Den Abbeele. Manchester: Manchester University Press, 1988.

—— *The Inhuman: Reflections on Time*, trans. Geoffrey Bennington and Rachel Bowlby. Oxford: Blackwell, 1991.

—— *Peregrinations: Law, Form, Event*. New York:

Columbia University Press, 1988.

—— *The Postmodern Condition: A Report on Knowledge*, trans. Geoffrey Bennington and Brian Massumi. Manchester: Manchester University Press, 1984.

Plant, Sadie, *Zeros + Ones: Digital Women + the New Technoculture*. London: Fourth Estate, 1997.

Sim, Stuart, (ed.), *The Critical Dictionary of Postmodern Thought*. Cambridge: Icon Books, 1998.

—— *Derrida and the End of History*. Cambridge: Icon Books, 1999.

—— *Modern Cultural Theorists: Jean-François Lyotard*. Hemel Hempstead: Prentice Hall, 1996.

Simpson, Roderick, 'The Brain Builder', *Wired*, 5 December 1997, pp. 234–5.

Ward, Mark, *Virtual Organisms: The Startling World of Artificial Life*. London: Macmillan, 1999.

Key Ideas

Artificial Intelligence (AI)
AI takes two main forms: systems that attempt to replicate human intelligence by means of a central processing mechanism standing in for the brain, and systems that 'learn' as they go, developing ever greater capacity for adaptability to new situations (as in the case of 'neural nets'). The more sophisticated the latter becomes, the more it takes on the characteristics of **Artificial Life** (**AL**).

Artificial Life (AL)
AL can refer to either robots or computer programs. In each case, the requirement is that the 'organism' becomes independent of human control, and 'evolves' in some recognisable manner. Evolution can be seen in programs such as the 'Game of Life', where we can observe new 'organisms' come into being from the relatively simple state (and set of rules) in operation at the program's start. Although the player can set the initial state of the 'Game' (specifying some 'live' and 'dead' cells on the game's infinite square grid), once it is under way he or she has no more input and the cells evolve

73

into an array of different 'species'. As the science writer Mark Ward has noted, the game's critical feature is that it is 'capable of producing an ever-growing pattern' (*Virtual Organisms*, p. 91).

Artilects

The **AI** theorist Hugo de Garis's term for massively more powerful AI systems, which can be thought of as 'Artificial Intellects'. When developed, these will far outstrip human intellects, and become coveted resources – to the point, de Garis predicts, of triggering political conflict.

Complexity Theory

Complexity represents the next generation of physical theory to chaos, and emphasises the role of self-organisation in systems – ranging from the human through to the entire universe. Systems are seen to be capable of evolution, and of achieving higher levels of development through spontaneous self-organisation. According to complexity theorists, emergent processes within systems are all that are needed to explain the occurrence of such phenomena, the occurrence of which is widespread.

Cyberspace

The 'space' in which computer programs operate, where the Internet is located, and across which your e-mail is transmitted. The term was coined by the science-fiction author William Gibson in his novel *Neuromancer*, which envisages a world where human beings can enter this 'virtual' space and match their wits against **AI**s. To quote *The Critical Dictionary of Postmodern Thought*, cyberspace 'is a non-space that is everywhere and yet nowhere' ('Cyberspace' entry, p. 219).

Cyborg

Donna Haraway's conception of a form of being combining the human and the technological. The point of such a construct is to break free of gender constraints, and of a social context where women are often regarded as biologically inferior beings to men. Cyborgs harness the power of machines to problematise such notions, as well as overcoming the limitations of the human body. Moreover, such close co-operation exists between humans and machines in the contemporary world, that Haraway contends that cyborg society is already a reality.

Development

Jean-François Lyotard's term for advanced capitalism (and such high-profile aspects of this phenomenon as the multinationals), whose sole concern is with expansion of its operations. Such expansion demands continual improvement of the system's productive efficiency, hence the appropriation of **techno-science** in its cause.

Enlightenment Project

The name given to the cultural movement that began in the eighteenth century, whose aim was to emphasise the role of reason in human affairs (earlier generations of historians often referred to it as the 'Age of Reason'). Such ideas underpin modernity, with its cult of progress based on the application of human reason to the task of dominating the environment around us, and thereby improving the human lot materially. Since the advent of postmodernism (and such aspects of that phenomenon as the emergence of the 'green movement') this cultural ethos has come under increasing attack, although it is still deeply engrained in our thinking in the 'developed' countries – not least among the professional political class.

Heat Death

A star such as our sun (a 'dwarf G star' so-called), goes through a life-cycle that involves it becoming hotter and hotter until it burns out – the phenomenon known as 'heat death'. According to current projections, this should happen somewhere between 4.5 billion and 6 billion years from now, although life will most likely have disappeared from earth long before that point as a result of the sun's increasing heat making conditions intolerable. Heat death is a consequence of the second law of thermodynamics, which asserts that closed systems (such as the universe) naturally gravitate towards a state of maximum entropy, or equilibrium, as the heat given off by objects within them dissipates throughout the entire system. The process, whereby hot flows to cold, is irreversible, and our sun is going through it.

Humanism

Humanism has a long history that can be traced back at least as far as classical Greece. In its modern formulation, it is essentially a product of the Renaissance, which involved an increasing interest in the individual and his or her capacity for self-development: 'man as the measure of all things' and so on. Humanism lies at the heart of the **Enlightenment Project** and modernity as a cultural phenomenon, and, as such, has come in for heavy criticism from the postmodern movement.

Inhumanism

Inhumanism is a blanket term designed to cover all those cases where the human dimension is eclipsed by the technological, or taken to be subsidiary to it in some way. To be an inhumanist is to be in favour of blurring the division between man and machine, as in the case of Donna Haraway's **cyborg** construct.

Post-humanism

The state many theorists claim that we are now in, where humanist values are no longer taken to be the norm and are even openly contested. A post-humanist society regards humanist ideals with scepticism, and is prone to see their negative side only (for example, the Holocaust as a logical extension of the humanist desire to find rational 'solutions' to all perceived social and political 'problems').

Techno-science

A term used by Jean-François Lyotard in *The Inhuman* to describe the range of forces committed to extending the domain of technology at the expense of humanity and its values. The hand of **development** (advanced capitalism, the multinationals) can be detected behind such an imperative, the main concern of which is to exert domination over an increasingly hostile environment by a massive increase in system efficiency.

Acknowledgements

My thanks to Dr Helene Brandon for advice on the medical examples used in the course of the argument.